Are you ready for an Art Attack?

Give Christmas some added sparkle by adding an Art Attack twist! You can make cards, gifts, decorations, crackers and festive table settings. I've shown you how to get started, now try it yourself!

If you're ready to have some tive fun turn the page and have some Art Attacks!

CONTENTS

4 Dear Santa

6 Advent tree

8 Santa sign

10 All wrapped up

12 Partridge in a pear tree

14 Get cracking

15 Take your place

18 Deer deer

19 Christmas cards

22 Snow family

24 Dazzling decorations

26 Hints and tips

Editor: Karen Brown   Designer: James Arnott and Jo England
Model Maker: Susie Johns

DEAR SANTA CLAUS...

WE KNOW CHRISTMAS IS NOT ABOUT THE PRESENTS BUT YOU MIGHT AS WELL LET SANTA KNOW WHAT YOU WOULD LIKE!

Dear Santa,
please may I have....

basketball boots
a pro skateboard
baseball cap
new pencil case
watercolour pencils

Merry Christmas!
with love from:- Sam
Address:-
2 Orchard crescent

YOU WILL NEED:

Plain paper, scissors, glue, felt tip pens.

1 Photocopy the letter on the opposite page on to white paper, then stick it on to a piece of thicker paper.

2 Trim the edges and colour everything in. Make sure the area where you will write is in a pale colour like yellow.

3 Write your letter to Santa - don't forget to add your address!

Photocopy the page several times and get everyone in your family to write a letter to Santa!

Dear Santa,
please may I have....

Merry Christmas!
with love from:-
Address:-

ADVENT TREE

COUNT DOWN TO CHRISTMAS DAY WITH THIS ART ATTACK
ADVENT TREE. START EACH DAY WITH A TINY TREAT!

1 On a large piece of thick card, draw a narrow triangle as your tree shape. Cut this out and paint it green.

2 Paint your toilet rolls in different colours or cover them with shiny wrapping paper and then cut them in half. You should have 24 halves.

3 Glue each half to the tree shape, using the picture as a guide. Pop a sweet or tiny gift into each half and then cover with a circle of tissue paper and glue in place.

4 Starting at the bottom, using 3D paint, write a number on top of each one from 1 to 24. Finally cut out a silver star and stick it to the top.

MAKE AN ADVENT TREE AS A GIFT AND FILL IT WITH THEIR FAVOURITE SWEETS!

ART ATTACK

7

SANTA SIGN!

You may have been good this year, but it wouldn't hurt to give Santa a helping hand! Remind him where you live with this super sign!

1 Cut out a large Father Christmas shape from cardboard box card. Cut out fingers, a beard and a brim for the hat as well.

2 Glue them in position. As you glue the fingers in place, stick a drinking straw in between the fingers and the backing card. Cut out a circle of card and stick it to the drinking straw to make the sign.

3 Mix 1 part PVA glue to 1 part water. Dip crumpled kitchen roll into the mixture and press on to the beard and brim. Cover the whole thing with two layers of papier maché and leave it to dry.

4 Now decorate with poster paints or acrylics and stick a cottonwool ball on the end of his hat. Finally write a message on the sign.

Cardboard box card, scissors, drinking straw, newspaper, kitchen roll, PVA glue, black marker pen, paint.

Santa
please
STOP
HERE!

All Wrapped Up!

FORGET EXPENSIVE WRAPPING PAPER - MAKE YOUR OWN! THE COLOURS, PATTERNS AND PRINTS THAT YOU CAN PRODUCE ARE ENDLESS.

1 You can use all sorts of different things to make prints - corks, erasers, potato, the wrong end of a pencil, or shop-bought rubber stamps.

2 Just dip your chosen 'stamper' into a shallow dish of paint or ink and press it on to the surface of the paper.

3 Repeat all over the surface of the paper, in straight lines or in a random pattern.

CUT LETTERS OR SHAPES FROM BITS OF SPONGE AND STICK THEM ON TO THICK CARD OR AN EMPTY MATCHBOX.

Sheets of paper – coloured or plain or even brown parcel paper, card, paints, ink, things to make shapes from such as potatoes, sponges or thick card.

MAKE MORE DETAILED PRINTS BY GLUING PIECES OF STRING TO A CARD BLOCK. THESE ARE GREAT AS YOU CAN USE THEM OVER AND OVER AGAIN.

BRIGHT IDEAS!

Instead of dipping your 'stamper' into paint, dip it into a puddle of PVA glue, print and then sprinkle with glitter while it's still wet!

Use shaped fruit such as star fruit, pears or mushrooms. Simply cut them in half. Carefully cut a shape into a potato half.

11

PARTRIDGE IN A PEAR TREE

THIS WILL GET YOU IN THE MOOD TO SING CHRISTMAS CAROLS!

YOU WILL NEED:
Plastic pot
stones
card
newspaper
sticky tape
pipe cleaners
paint
green tissue

1

Half fill a plastic flower pot with stones to weigh it down. Cut a circle of card with a hole in the middle to fit in the top. Roll up a sheet of newspaper into a tight tube, push it into the hole and secure with sticky tape.

2

To make branches, use pipe cleaners wrapped around the main stem. Wrap each pipe cleaner with sticky tape.

3

To make the pears, crumple sheets of newspaper tightly into balls. Bind with sticky tape, shaping them into pear shapes as you go. Stick a short length of pipe cleaner into the ends.

To make the partridge, shape the body in the same way as the pears. Add a tube of card for the neck, a smaller paper ball for the head, and a tail and beak cut from card. Stick on legs made from pipe cleaners.

5 Cover everything with three layers of papier maché and leave to dry. Do not cover the partridge's feet.

6 Paint the tree, the pears and the partridge. Use blobs of PVA glue to stick the pears to the branches. Secure the partridge using the pipe cleaner feet and some glue. Finally stick on some green tissue leaves.

GET CRACKING

MAKE CHRISTMAS DINNER REALLY
SPECIAL BY MAKING A CRACKER
FOR EVERYONE AT THE TABLE!

1 Cut out a rectangle of tissue or crepe paper.

2 Place a small toy or sweet in a toilet roll tube. Add a silly joke, even a paper hat!

3 Wrap the tissue around the toilet roll tube and stick in place.

4 Tie each end with string or ribbon.

5 Decorate the cracker and stick on names made from coloured paper or card.

YOU CAN USE THIS
KIND OF WRAPPING FOR A
LARGER GIFT TO PUT
UNDER THE TREE.

ROLL CORRUGATED CARD
INTO A TUBE SHAPE AND
COVER IT WITH GIFT
WRAPPING INSTEAD.

14

ART ATTACK

TAKE YOUR PLACE

BRIGHTEN UP THE FESTIVE FEAST WITH THESE COLOURFUL PLACE MATS AND YULETIDE NAPKIN RINGS!

YOU WILL NEED:

Plain paper
scissors
felt tip pens

NAPKINS

1. Over the page you will find your napkin rings. Simply photocopy the page on to plain paper.

2. Stick them on to thin card and colour them in using felt tip pens.

3. Cut the napkin rings out. Make a slit where marked on each end and fold into place.

PLACEMATS

1. Over the page you will also find your placemats. Photocopy the mat as many times as you need.

2. Stick it on to thin card and colour it in using your felt tip pens or paints.

3. Trim the mat to fit and then cover with sticky backed plastic.

THINK OF OTHER THINGS YOU CAN MAKE FOR THE TABLE - WHAT ABOUT PLACE CARDS OR MENUS?

DEER, DEER!

DECORATE THE HOUSE WITH THESE EASY-TO-MAKE FESTIVE REINDEER.

YOU WILL NEED:

Pencil and paper
cardboard
glue
scissors
pipe cleaner
paints
red pom pom
googly eyes

1 Photocopy or trace the templates below on to paper. Cut out one of each shape.

2 Draw around the templates on to card. You will need one head, one body, one neck, one tail and two legs.

3 Cut the pieces and out and decorate. You could even stick sequins all over the body.

4 Cut slits where marked and fit the pieces together. Stick on googly eyes, pipe cleaner antlers and a red pom pom nose.

YOU CAN MAKE AS MANY REINDEER AS YOU LIKE - DECORATE THEM IN ALL DIFFERENT COLOURS.

18

CHRISTMAS CARDS!

CHRISTMAS WOULDN'T BE THE SAME WITHOUT CARDS. CHECK OUT THE CREATIVE 3D CARDS OVER THE PAGE AND MAKE A LIST SO YOU DON'T FORGET ANY ONE!

YOU WILL NEED:

To make the card list: plain paper, scissors, glue, felt tip pens.

To make cards: Thin coloured card, scissors, glue, craft foam, sequins, fake fur, coloured card, glitter, tinsel.

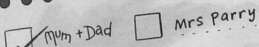

CHRISTMAS CARD LIST

- [✓] Mum + Dad
- [ ] Mrs Parry
- [✓] gran
- [ ] Carol and Ken
- [✓] Uncle Mike + Auntie Jean
- [ ] Uncle Jim
- [✓] Maureen and Phil
- [ ] Mr. Poole
- [✓] Karen
- [ ] Mr. and Mrs. Ellison
- [✓] Paul
- [ ] Bob
- [✓] Best friend

Turn to page 20 to find your card list. Photocopy this page on to plain paper.

Stick it on to thin card and trim it to fit.

Colour the list in and write all the names of the people for whom you are going to make cards.

HOW ABOUT MAKING A LIST FOR EACH MEMBER OF THE FAMILY?

FUN FOAM

How about cutting shapes from card, paper or craft foam. Make them stand out from the background by using sticky pads or small pieces of card between the backing and the shape.

Write festive messages or decorate with dimensional paints for a fab, colourful 3D effect.

Creative Collage

Make unique christmas cards by sticking scrap paper, decorations, even an old CD on the front of coloured card.

Sequins and glitter also add a brilliant 3D effect to cards and give a wonderful sparkle.

TERRIFIC TEXTURE

Make your Father Christmas and reindeer cards stand out by giving them a textured make over. How about a balloon or pom pom nose, fake fur and googly eyes? You could even make mini versions as matching gift tags.

3D paints are very effective - these paints come in small bottles with fine nozzles for writing and decorating.

Snow Family!

TOO COLD TO GO OUTSIDE BUT
STILL WANT TO BUILD SNOWMEN?
HOW ABOUT THIS CHILLED OUT
SNOW FAMILY?

1

Blow up three balloons to three different sizes for bodies. Blow up three smaller balloons for heads. Cover with at least eight layers of papier maché and leave to dry.

2

Burst the balloons and trim the bases of each body. Stick a circle of card in place to make a flat bottom. Tape a ring of card onto the bodies for necks, then stick the heads in place. Stick on tiny card cones for noses and rolled up paper for arms.

YOU WILL NEED:

❄ 6 BALLOONS ❄ NEWSPAPER
❄ PVA GLUE ❄ STICKY TAPE ❄
CARDBOARD ❄ KITCHEN ROLL
❄ PAINTS ❄ GOOGLY EYES

3

To make the hats, cut two circles of card, one smaller than the other. Cut a hole in the larger one to fit on the snowman's head. Secure the two circles together with a ring of card in between. Stick these on the heads.

4

For a bobble hat, stick a ball of paper on the head and a sausage of paper round the head for the brim. Cover the snowmen with another two layers of papier maché and leave to dry throughly before painting. Finally stick on googly eyes.

DAZZLING DECORATIONS!

Stick a paper clip to a piece of thick, round card. Cover it with a layer of papier mâché and let it dry. Paint, and attach it to a piece of ribbon.

Thread beads on to pipe cleaners. Bend the pipe cleaners to form a large star shape.

You may need to join several pipe cleaners together.

Wrap a small box with shiny paper and tie it with ribbon. Make a small gift tag from a scrap of card.

H Chri

YOU WILL NEED:

Pipe cleaners, beads, polystyrene egg shape, sequins, pins, small box, silver paper, coloured paper, ribbon, glue, scissors, string.

HAVE AN ART ATTACK AND DECORATE THE HOUSE AND THE CHRISTMAS TREE. HERE ARE A FEW IDEAS - MAKE UP SOME OF YOUR OWN.

Cut two identical star shapes from silver card. Cut a slit in each one, from a point to the centre and slot together.

Make a hole in the top and thread with a piece of ribbon to hang up.

Start with a polystyrene egg. Push a short pin through a tiny bead, then through a sequin and into the egg. Repeat until the whole surface is covered with sequins.

Finally make a hanging loop by pinning a length of ribbon to the top.

To make a starburst, start by folding a long rectangle of coloured paper and make concertina folds along its length.

Tie a piece of thread around the middle and open it out, gluing the ends together to form a circle.

HiNTS AND TiPS!

USiNG GLiTTER

Various different types of glue can be used with glitter. A glue stick or PVA are good for large areas. For fine details, choose PVA in a small bottle with a fine nozzle, or a dimensional fabric paint.

Glitter is available in lots of colours and different grades, from fine to quite coarse.

FANCY DRESS PARTY

CHRISTMAS

PAPiER MACHE

When you combine paper and glue you can make some very exciting - and surprisingly sturdy - models.

Save old newspapers, which are perfect for most models. Finer details are easier if you use tissue paper, kitchen towel or toilet paper. PVA is the best glue to use - you will need to dilute it with water to make a runny consistency.

PAiNTS

When buying paints, you only need a few colours to start with - blue, red, yellow, white and black - any other colours can be mixed.

Poster paints are great for painting pictures and papier maché models. They are available in small pots, and tubes which are called 'gouache.' Larger bottles of ready mixed poster paint are good for larger paintings and big models. You can also use acrylic paints.